My

Written by
Diana Noonan

Illustrated by
Wendy Smith-Griswold

Celebration Press
An Imprint of Pearson Learning

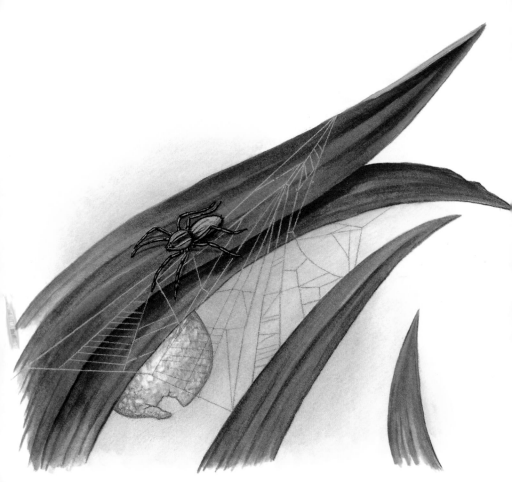

My nest is in the grass.

My nest is in the sand.

My nest is in the mud.

My nest is in the hay.

My nest is in the tree.

My nest is in the hole.

My nest is on Dad's feet!